BUNGALOW BASICS
DINING ROOMS

By Paul Duchscherer
Photography by Douglas Keister

Pomegranate

SAN FRANCISCO

Published by Pomegranate Communications, Inc.
Box 808022, Petaluma, California 94975
800-227-1428; www.pomegranate.com

Pomegranate Europe Ltd.
Unit 1, Heathcote Business Centre, Hurlbutt Road
Warwick, Warwickshire CV34 6TD, U. K.
(44) 01926 430111

Library of Congress Cataloging-in-Publication Data
Duchscherer, Paul.
    Bungalow basics. Dining rooms / by Paul Duchscherer ; photography by
Douglas Keister.
        p. cm.
    ISBN 0-7649-2493-1
    1. Bungalows. 2. Dining rooms. 3. Arts and crafts movement–United States.
I. Title: Dining rooms. II. Keister, Douglas. III. Title.

    NA7571.D822 2003
    728'.373–dc21

                                                                    2003042985

Pomegranate Catalog No. A677

Designed by Patrice Morris

Printed in Korea

12 11 10 09 08 07 06 05 04 03   10 9 8 7 6 5 4 3 2 1

This book is dedicated to the discovery,
appreciation, and preservation of bungalows,
and especially to all those who
love and care for them.

Acknowledgments

Because of space limitations, we regret that it is not possible to acknowledge each of those individuals and organizations who have helped us with this book. Our heartfelt appreciation is extended especially to all the homeowners who, by graciously sharing their homes with us, have made this book a reality. Special thanks are given also to Sandy Schweitzer, John Freed, and Don Merrill for their tireless support, unflagging encouragement, and invaluable assistance. We salute you!

At the end of the book, we have noted a few of the talented artisans, architects, designers, craftspeople, and manufacturers whose work appears here, but space constraints preclude us from crediting each one. We offer them all our deepest gratitude. Alternatively, our readers may wish to consult the extensive credit listings in our earlier book series, published by Penguin Putnam Inc. (comprising *The Bungalow: America's Arts & Crafts Home, Inside the Bungalow: America's Arts & Crafts Interior*, and *Outside the Bungalow: America's Arts & Crafts Garden*), which make reference to many of the images that are also included in this book.

T he early twentieth century was a pivotal time for Americans. New technology was evolving at a spiraling rate; change, it seemed, was everywhere. For the middle class, especially the younger, more mobile generation, it was a time of unprecedented opportunities. A goal for many was to find a new home, preferably one that was not only affordable but more practical than the Victorian-era houses in which they had been raised. Yet few were willing to entirely relinquish the near-sacred domestic rituals that they had cherished. For most, the need and desire for a dining room were as strong as ever; the room itself just needed a bit of a makeover.

As Americans discovered the convenience, practicality, and charm of the bungalow (touted as the most modern house of the day), prospective homeowners enthused that its designers and builders were actually listening to their wants and needs. Although the bungalow was indeed a new and more efficient kind of house, one of its most appealing aspects was its rather traditional emphasis on the dining room, a carryover from the preceding era. Dining rooms had long enjoyed status as a primary "public" room in most American houses, but their presence in bungalows was amplified by greater visibility and interaction with adjoining rooms, chiefly the living room. Because bungalows were planned with little wasted space, long hallways were largely eliminated, with the major rooms used as circulation space instead. Thus, rather than being separate, sequestered areas, the bungalow's dining and living rooms were constantly traversed in the comings and goings of family activities. Kept as open to each other as possible, these two rooms together usually constituted about half the square footage of the entire house, creating a very spacious effect in many plans (Figures 4–6, 10).

Most associated with bungalows today, the Craftsman style peaked in popularity about the time of World War I. By then, it had produced some of the most classic examples of bungalow design and planning ingenuity. Separate from their furnishings or even their decorative schemes, the architectural elements of dining rooms of this time have certain definitive features. What first comes to mind are the distinctive wall divisions created by paneling called a wainscot. In this period, wainscoting rose higher on the wall than the chair-rail height of previous eras and routinely was capped by a narrow display shelf, called a plate rail (Figures 4, 7). Wainscots were usually detailed in board-and-batten fashion, utilizing narrow, vertical wood strips (battens) to cover the joint lines of wide, flat boards set side by side (vertically). Most wainscots tended to be quite simply detailed, with perhaps an extra horizontal line or two of narrow molding just below the plate rail (Figure 8). Issues of cost and fashion sometimes dictated the use of battens only, allowing space for decorative painted finishes or wall coverings between them in lieu of wood (Figures 1–3, 25, 32–33). Most dining room wainscots were about two-thirds of the overall wall height, which reinforced the horizontal room proportions associated with Craftsman-style bungalows.

The height of the wall space remaining above the wainscot determined the kind of decorative wall treatment that would be most suitable. Rooms whose wainscot extended close to the ceiling had space for only a narrow border. The more typical wainscot height allowed space for a wider border, called a frieze (most commonly of wallpaper), which made a bolder design statement (Figures 30–43, 46, 48). Friezes often featured nature motifs; landscape friezes were popular Craftsman-era choices (Figures 31–34, 40–42). However, the most prevalent patterns for dining room friezes employed some variation of the grapevine motif (Figures 35–37) or that of grapes mixed with other fruit (Figures 38–39). Some walls above wainscots were wallpapered with an overall pattern yet still had room for a border or a frieze (Figures 28, 44). Other walls were given special hand-painted finishes that might utilize sponging or ragging techniques to add texture (Figure 17); sometimes multiple colors were blended to produce a "Tiffany finish" (Figure 2). Another possibility was stenciling, which could be combined with other paint treatments to create patterned friezes (Figure 30) and smaller borders. Occasionally a simple woven material like grass cloth (Figure 15) or a textile like plain linen or burlap (Figure 13) was used as an overall wall covering, or a patterned textile could serve as a frieze (Figures 40–42). Sometimes dining room walls were simply painted, generally in a warm, earthy color palette that harmonized with the surrounding woodwork (Figures 5, 12, 29).

Flooring in bungalow dining rooms was typically hardwood (usually oak), with area carpets used under most dining tables and chairs. "Fitted" (wall-to-wall) carpeting was out of fashion during the period. In some houses, hardwood floors featured contrasting border strips, which might have decorative corner flourishes (Figure 26). Other hard-surface materials, like tile (Figure 22), were rarely used. Some homes utilized practical linoleum, which at the time was available in so-called rug patterns, installed with hardwood flooring at the dining room's perimeter (Figure 25). Machine-made or hand-knotted Oriental rugs were the more usual choices; period images also show the use of plain-field rugs with simple borders, a more "modern" choice (Figures 1–2, 33).

In terms of woodwork and finish, bungalows typically featured a less expensive wood (like fir) that was darkly stained to conceal any uneven figuring in its grain (Figure 5). Stained woodwork typically appeared in the main rooms, but the woodwork in the "private" and "utility" areas of the house was often painted a "hygienic" pale cream or white. Original decorating schemes that used light-colored painted woodwork for the primary rooms (Figure 37) were more common in the 1920s and, if accompanied by classical moldings, indicative of a Colonial Revival influence.

Revealed structure was a hallmark of Arts and Crafts design, and beamed ceilings became a major component in many dining rooms before the 1920s. In reality the ceiling beams in most bungalows were not necessarily holding anything up. True structural beams did appear occasionally (Figures 6, 26–27), but usually in custom-built, architect-designed homes rather than in typical bungalows. Most common were box beams (constructed like hollow boxes), which at first glance appeared to be structural. The undersides of box beams were often slightly recessed, and small moldings were frequently used to cover up their point of contact with the ceiling.

The configuration of box-beamed ceilings varied widely: some framed the room's perimeter (Figures 24, 29, 30); some went in only one direction (Figures 9, 10, 19, 40); and some covered the ceiling with a large grid (Figures 7, 33, 48). Depending on a dining room's proportions and orientation, some beamed ceiling layouts matched that of the adjoining living room, while others manipulated the room's sense of space and scale with an entirely different arrangement. An oversized crown molding could serve to anchor the room's perimeter (Figures 4, 8, 14, 20). Another option was to stop all woodwork at the top of the wainscot, leaving the plastered wall and ceiling space for paint or wallpaper treatments (Figures 1, 21, 46).

Dining room lighting needed to be less "atmospheric" than that in the living room and more functional. This meant that the dining table, within easy view (or earshot) of a parent in the kitchen or living room, was a well-lit and convenient place for the children of the household to do their homework. More decorative lighting, such as wall sconces, also appeared in dining rooms (Figures 12, 28, 43, 46). One possible effect with a ceiling that featured crossing box beams was to place accent lighting at each intersection. The fixture styles for this arrangement could vary from bare lightbulbs set flush to the beams (Figure 3) to small lanterns suspended from chains (Figure 29). Lantern-style fixtures were available in many sizes and could be boxy or cylindrical in shape, but they usually featured art-glass shades. Fixtures made from glass bowls suspended on chains were also a popular source of general lighting (Figures 4, 12). Another fixture style, called a shower, was made up of several smaller lanterns hanging—sometimes at different heights—from a single ceiling-mounted backplate. These lanterns could be set in a line above a long rectangular table, a configuration promoted by Gustav Stickley (Figures 20, 30). Most of these fixture styles are being reproduced by numerous manufacturers today.

Another key element of dining rooms, subject to several different design treatments, was one shared (literally) with the living room: the opening between them. These openings tended to be at least as wide as a double door and were often somewhat wider (Figures 10–11). A popular treatment was to have the openings fitted with sliding pocket doors. In the 1920s, it became common (and less expensive) to employ French doors between the dining and living rooms. These doors admitted light and allowed visual connection when closed but required "swing space" to open, thus limiting the options for arranging furniture. Although some dining and living rooms were originally designed as a single undivided space, this scheme was more often the result of a later remodel (Figure 17).

A popular way to separate dining and living rooms was with a colonnade, which consisted of a pair of columns supported by low walls set within a wide opening (Figure 5). The shapes of the columns varied considerably, but the Craftsman style favored tapered, square, or trapezoidal shapes. Turned, rounded columns with a classical look sometimes appeared in houses with a Colonial Revival influence. Often the low walls that supported the columns incorporated built-in bookcases or display cabinets (which usually opened toward the living room). In a more open variation of the colonnade concept, columns were deleted, but the low walls or built-in cabinets were retained (Figures 3–4).

Although they did not fit into colonnades, portières (doorway draperies) were a popular textile treatment employed to soften the hard edges of wide doorway openings (Figure 2). They also blocked unwanted drafts, muffled sound, and provided privacy without the need for closing any doors. Sometimes portières featured different fabrics on each side, if adjoining decorating schemes varied. Many bungalows still have traces of hanging hardware that once supported portières within doorways. A carryover from the Victorian era, they remain a sensible decorating idea today and are enjoying a well-deserved revival.

The built-in called the sideboard (or buffet), which dominates most bungalow dining rooms, was usually the most substantial—and arguably the most useful—built-in feature of the house. Like most other bungalow built-ins, sideboards typically were obtained from catalogs by builders rather than being made on-site at greater cost. However, this certainly did not restrict the variety, beauty, and ingenuity of designs that were produced and survive in great numbers. To save valuable space, most sideboards were designed to be recessed so that their fronts were flush to the face of the wall (Figures 3–4, 7–8, 14, 22, 25, 29, 44). Depending on the architectural layout, this recessed effect might be achieved by cantilevering the sideboard off the side of the house (in the manner of a bay window). When there was no other option, the sideboard was installed to project into the room, almost like a freestanding piece of furniture (Figures 23–24).

Despite the many unique variations of sideboard designs, the basic configuration of most sideboards was fairly similar. Below an open serving surface (which doubled as a display space), most had enclosed storage space that included a combination of cupboards (usually with solid-panel doors) for larger serving pieces and several drawers for silverware and linens. To reflect light back into the room and enhance the objects (or edibles) on display, a beveled mirrored panel frequently appeared behind the serving surface. Some possessed the added convenience of having their back panels lift or slide to expose a step-saving "pass-through" opening to the kitchen, which was otherwise reachable through a nearby swinging door (Figure 22). The upper, more visible part of the sideboard had cabinets made for storage and display of china and crystal pieces, which could be admired through cabinet doors inset with beveled, leaded, or art-glass panels.

A row of windows along one side of a dining room was a fairly common bungalow feature (Figure 8). These were sometimes set into a shallow bay that accommodated a long built-in window seat below them. Such a window seat was typically constructed with a lift-up top, for access to a storage area. To save floor space, the shallow bay with the window seat was made to project off the side of the house, like some sideboards.

Furnishing the dining room was a reasonably simple matter. If a built-in sideboard was present, a dining table and chairs might have been all the furniture that was needed (or that could fit comfortably). As the Craftsman style went out of fashion, so did its preponderance of built-ins; many later bungalows were purposefully designed without them. However, plenty of earlier houses lacked them too, considering the large number of freestanding sideboards and other serving pieces that were made to match Craftsman-style dining tables and chairs (Figures 1, 48). By the 1920s, a fashion for coordinated sets (or "suites") of dining furniture, many of dubious design quality, was sweeping the middle class. Most favored by then were vaguely historic styles, inspired by seventeeth- and eighteeth-century designs, reflecting the growing Colonial Revival influence that eclipsed the Craftsman style.

Although bungalow dining rooms tended to be quite roomy, they usually did not have enough space around the perimeter to comfortably accommodate a working fireplace. Sometimes dining rooms shared a view of the living room's fireplace (Figures 5, 11, 17). A few dining rooms incorporated practical gas heaters within scaled-down mantels, and some higher-budget homes did have full-sized dining room fireplaces (Figures 16, 43, 46).

The bungalow dining room's central location, and its traditional role as the family's primary gathering place for daily meals, made it the true heart of the home. Over dinner table conversations, it was the place where family members kept abreast of each other's trials and tribulations and discussed the triumphs and tragedies of the world. Those living in a bungalow today find that the dining room is still the heart of their home. Bungalow living can help remind us that dreams of domestic bliss still echo deep in our collective memory; although times have changed, our basic daily wants and needs have not.

1. This dining room appeared in a 1910 catalog called *Handcraft Furniture*, by L. and J. G. Stickley; it reappeared in a 1912 design advice book entitled *Home Building and Decoration*, by Henry Collins Brown. The matching gray-green stain recommended for both the furniture and woodwork was an idea that also interested Gustav Stickley, but the potential of such colored wood stains was limited by their tendency to fade.

2. This room design, published in 1910 by the Sherwin-Williams Paint Company in *Your Home and Its Decoration,* was intended to show how a variety of painted finishes could replace any need for wallpaper. Above a high wainscot, the frieze is stenciled with Art Nouveau-style plant forms. The multihued effect sponged into the panels below was sometimes called a "Tiffany finish." Textiles (bordered carpet, chair upholstery, table runner, and portière) reinforce the green-and-amber color scheme.

🐝 3. This spacious dining room has very shallow box beams, with intentionally bare lightbulbs at each intersection, a vestige of a time when unshielded electric lighting still had decorative appeal. The opening in the foreground (to the living room) has two low walls to either side that function as display surfaces. Next to a swinging door to the kitchen, a built-in sideboard with leaded glass doors aligns with the plate rail of the adjacent high wainscot.

🐾 4. Between dining and living rooms from 1913, a pair of built-in pedestals, resembling stairway newel posts, display pottery. Allowing direct access to a covered side porch, a pair of French doors and sidelights, each framed in colored glass, admit a mellow light. Flanked by tall pilasters, an unusual built-in sideboard with geometric art-glass doors is the dining room's focal point. Recessed above is a beveled mirror, angled to give diners a view of the table.

☙ 5. Builders commonly ordered colonnades, like the one seen here, from a catalog, along with other typical prefabricated built-ins (such as the window seat that opens for storage, at right). This example has bookcases with glass doors on the other side, facing into the living room. The colonnade maintains some views of the fireplace from the dining room. Above it, at far left, the front door is partly visible.

🐨 6. This 1906 Berkeley, California, home's rough-hewn wood, massive exposed structural elements, and entirely open plan set it apart from most bungalows. In an unusual spatial arrangement, the living room wraps around two sides of the dining area. A two-step level change occurs in the foreground, allowing outlooks over the entire space from the table. A full-width, built-in sideboard has leaded glass cabinet doors aligned with recessed windows above.

❦ 7. A highlight of this 1907 bungalow dining room is its collection of period art pottery, including a group of colorful plates in Royal Doulton's Poppy pattern, displayed on a plate rail that caps the high board-and-batten wainscoting. Recessed into the wainscot, to the left of the sideboard, is a "bonus" built-in storage cupboard. Also still in place are original copper-and-glass lighting fixtures. A freestanding Charles Stickley sideboard (at far left) offers additional storage and display spaces.

❦ 8. *(overleaf)* This dining room has very simple yet strong linear woodwork and detailing, typical of the Craftsman style, which appeals to many today because of its almost "protomodern" quality. Perhaps budget limitations prompted the builder to make the wainscot and plate rail lower in height than most others and, instead of box beams, to use deeply coved crown molding.

🐾 9. *(above)* This all-redwood dining room, dating to 1899, is a result of a progressive design movement that blossomed in the San Francisco Bay Area around the turn of the last century. Lilian Bridgman, a friend of renowned local architect Bernard Maybeck, designed and built this house for herself. The dining table, pulled up to a built-in bench that runs the entire length of the room, was also designed by Bridgman.

🐨 10. The Craftsman-style interior of the 1907 Corbett House in Tucson, Arizona, is unexpected, considering its Mission Revival exterior. Recognizing its significance, the city of Tucson acquired the home in 1968, and it was restored and refurnished as a house museum by the Tucson Museum of Art. A judiciously appropriate infusion of at least some period color (pattern optional) would soften the contrast of dark wood and white walls.

🐾 11. A wide doorway provides this dining room with views of the living room and its fireplace. Long abused, this house was recently renovated, and many of its missing woodwork elements (including the box beams) were restored. The elegant art-glass ceiling fixture has matching sconces visible above the living room fireplace. English Arts and Crafts pieces include the stylish china cabinet and the dining chairs.

🐝 12. Overlooking a lush bamboo grove, the large windows of this 1909 dining room are flanked by wainscot-high built-in china cabinets. The small sideboard and the dining chairs are by Gustav Stickley, and the table is a Stickley Brothers piece. Rather than the usual box variety, these ceiling "beams" are made up of flat molding. The area at right, now enclosed with vintage English art-glass panels, was formerly part of an open front porch.

13. With a commanding view from its Hollywood hills perch, the dining room of "Mariposa" (formerly the Frost-Tufts house), designed by Arthur R. Kelly, was recently restored to near-original state. Natural burlap wall covering sets off the simple Craftsman detailing of the board-and-batten wainscot and box-beamed ceiling. The sun porch at left, once an outdoor terrace, was enclosed soon after the house was built in 1911.

14. With the usual arrangement of enclosed storage space below a wide serving surface backed by a mirrored panel, a built-in sideboard dominates the dining room of a Craftsman bungalow built in 1914. The upper china cabinet doors are inset with leaded glass panels. Out of view at right is a swinging door to the kitchen, which can also be accessed from the hallway visible through the door in the corner. A new Craftsman-style ceiling fixture mixes well with the Arts and Crafts-period furniture and a fine art pottery collection.

🐝 15. The built-in sideboard in this 1908 Pasadena, California, house, designed by architect Frederick Louis Roehrig, incorporates three windows between a pair of tall china cabinets with leaded glass doors. Its lower portion resembles a large desk, with "knee space" in the middle for a chair. A favorite period wall covering, grass cloth (used both above and below a plate rail shelf) adds warm, natural color and texture to the room.

🐝 16. The 1908 Gamble House, open to the public as a house museum, is the most famous of the masterworks created by renowned architects Charles and Henry Greene. Its high level of quality is evident in the dining room's mahogany paneling and inventive detailing. The fireplace tile surround has iridescent mosaic accents. Over the dining table, an imposing art-glass ceiling fixture hangs on leather straps. Backlit by a series of stunning art-glass panels, the built-in sideboard has a stepped form that recalls a Japanese *tansu* chest.

🐾 17. A recent bungalow renovation re-created many elements (such as the woodwork and fireplace mantel) that were lost to previous "modernizations." Despite the likelihood that some kind of architectural division once separated the dining and living rooms, the two areas were kept open as a single space; now only a large settle divides them. The period-style curtain treatments (matching the dining table's runner) and a select group of fine Arts and Crafts furnishings and lighting fixtures can all be enjoyed from either area.

18. As enthusiasm for the Craftsman style waned, the Spanish Colonial Revival style became a popular choice for bungalows by the 1920s. This San Diego dining room, in a 1927 house designed by local architect Richard Requa, has many features associated with that style: arched openings (fully rounded arches were also typical), corner fireplace, adobe-like textured walls, coved ceiling, decorative use of wrought iron, and dining furniture. Less typical is the small art-glass window at left.

🐚 19. Wide-swinging doors, inset with leaded and beveled glass panels, were used instead of the more typical pocket doors in the living/dining room doorway of a 1912 Craftsman home. A central stylized tulip motif relieves the linear, geometric glass design. Opposite the doorway, the built-in sideboard has an unusual mirrored treatment below its upper cabinet doors: a row of individual glass panels, each with a crinkly-textured ("crazed") mirrored finish, bordered with clear mirror.

20. The angled sideboard appears to be an integral part of the period woodwork of this 1909 dining room, but actually it is a recent re-creation. Based on outlines left by the missing original, its details are adapted from other examples of similar date and style. Backed with art glass, slender cutout shapes in the lower doors are repeated in the new swinging kitchen door at right.

🐝 21. A massive sideboard, nearly the length of the dining room in a 1914 bungalow, fits neatly into a wall between the swinging kitchen door (at right) and another door to a bedroom hall (out of view, at left). Behind a long serving/display surface, the mirrored panel reflects light and views back into the room. The stylized tulip motif in the leaded glass panels of the china cabinet doors is echoed in an art-glass panel on the kitchen door. Windows and French doors open to a patio with a vine-draped pergola. The dining table and chairs are Stickley reproductions.

✿ 22. The handles on the mirrored panel of this 1912 sideboard show that it slides up for a convenient "pass-through" to the kitchen. Columns of a colonnade (partly seen at left) are echoed in the pair of pilasters (mounted with original sconces) that frame the sideboard. Also original but unusual (outside a bathroom), the flooring of hexagonal porcelain tiles repeats in the bungalow's other main rooms.

23. This sideboard exudes a strong architectural quality: a pair of square posts rise from its serving surface to support a large crossbeam beneath the upper cabinets. Smaller beams (positioned like those on top of an outdoor pergola) elevate the angled cabinets for an airier effect. The cabinetry below has cutout accents, backed with green art glass, and original brass hardware. In a whimsical touch, iron chains stretch from the ends of the crossbeam, appearing to secure it to the upper wall behind.

🐝 24. Unlike most built-in sideboards, which are typically inset flush with the wall to conserve floor space, the one in the 1908 Charles Warren Brown House in Santa Monica, California, projects into the dining room like a piece of free-standing furniture. Backlit to either side by small windows, the sideboard also has an unusual open shelf above its upper cabinets. The square art-glass ceiling fixture has architectural lines consistent with those of the room.

25. Less typical of the Craftsman style, the vertical proportions of this sideboard were probably dictated by the rather high ceiling. Box beams and the wainscot's wall moldings help reduce the room's verticality. The warm upper wall color and the textured painting effect used in the wainscot panels re-create a period color scheme. A vintage linoleum "rug" with an overall floral pattern survives on the floor.

26 & 27. These views show a 1910 dining room that was part of a recent remodel that added a new kitchen (visible through the doorway at right in Figure 26) to the back of the house. The former kitchen has been converted to a den (also visible in Figure 26, to the left of the original built-in sideboard). Now facing the den, the old kitchen cabinet behind the sideboard remains, and the pass-through has been permanently opened for more visual access between the rooms. A new door (in the far corner of Figure 27), cleverly made

to resemble the adjacent casement windows, opens to a new outside deck. To its left, a built-in shelving unit awaits replacement of its original glass doors. Other features of the room include structural ceiling beams, a hefty plate rail (now displaying a basket collection) underscored by dentil molding, and inlaid borders in the hardwood floor with corner "knot" detailing, visible in Figure 26.

🐝 28. Because this house had suffered from insensitive "modernizations" over the years, most of the period-style woodwork in this dining room was re-created to match surviving elements. Set right above the plate rail, the wallpaper frieze adapts a period design by Englishman Walter Crane. Arts and Crafts-era furnishings and lighting prevail; on the table are crossing table runners, a period touch promoted by Gustav Stickley.

29. Quartersawn oak, typical of Craftsman furniture but less common for bungalow woodwork, inspired the muted orange paint above the plate rail in the restored dining room of the 1911 Keyes bungalow in Altadena, California. Painted a subtle grayish cream, the upper walls and box-beamed ceiling blend together. Period furnishings appear with reproduction lighting, including a central fixture of five small lanterns with pierced copper shades; matching lanterns punctuate crossing beams.

🐾 30. Fine period collectibles, including Gustav Stickley furniture, are arranged beneath shallow, crossing box beams in this 1912 dining room. Re-created here is a lighting concept proposed by Stickley: a row of small lanterns hanging, at staggered heights, from a wood backplate above the long table. The new stenciled frieze adapts the design of stylized plants in a period carpet border. Simple, banded linen curtains and crossing table runners are other Stickley-approved features.

31. In the style of California's early-twentieth-century *plein air* painters, the frieze in this 1912 Altadena, California, dining room encircles the room in a changing panorama. Recently hand-painted in place, it was inspired by the popular landscape friezes of the period (which typically were wallpaper designs with more stylized interpretations). Designed for this house by its architect, Harold Doolittle, the sideboard has a high open shelf instead of a serving surface.

❦ 32 & 33. From the 1914–1915 catalog of James Davis Artistic Paper Hangings, these two dining rooms both have large-scale landscape frieze designs that are best described as "scenics." Lithographed in Germany in the European tradition of mural-like scenic wallpapers, their Craftsman-style settings suggest that they were imported for the American market. More costly than the common roller-printed variety, lithographed wall coverings were more substantial in weight and had sharper resolution. The frieze in Figure 32 (above) depicts scenes of Rome; wainscot panels below have unpatterned, textured paper framed by narrow paper borders. The box-beamed dining room in Figure 33 makes a bolder landscape statement, with its panoramic views of woodsy mountain scenery. Below the plate rail, the wainscot employs a heavily textured paper background, divided by paper borders that descend from panels of stylized leaves (in the manner of a "pendant" frieze design).

❦ 34. *(overleaf, left)* The period-style elements of this 1905 dining room had already been removed before a fire occurred, which hastened the owners' previous intention to re-create them. The sideboard design was adapted from others found in neighboring homes. Leaded glass panels in its cabinet doors employ salvaged window glass for its wavy, aged look. Glazed a soft green, the painted wall finish harmonizes with both the tree-filled view through the French doors and the frieze, a reproduction of Walter Crane's Maytree pattern.

❧ 35. *(overleaf, right)* The original embossed wallpaper frieze in this 1915 bungalow dining room features a more delicate variation of the popular grapevine motif seen in Figure 36. Although machine-made, it was designed to resemble hand-tooled leather through its raised surface relief and richly reflective metallic inks. Restating the motif, the art-glass windows have grapes combined with oversized butterflies that show an Art Nouveau influence (curiously, the panel at right is upside-down). Also original are the all-wood box-beamed ceiling, built-in sideboard with simpler art-glass panels, and Colonial Revival-style lighting with a silvery finish.

❧ 36. *(right)* Set off by darkly stained woodwork, an original frieze survives in a 1907 dining room in Spokane, Washington. With still-striking results, it combines stenciling and hand-painted techniques in subtle colors, with a boldness of scale and pattern. A period favorite, its motif of intertwining grapes and vines was considered an appropriate choice for dining room schemes. Across the tops of the art-glass window panels, the spade-shaped forms suggest an English Arts and Crafts influence.

☙ 37. *(above, left)* Unlike most of the other rooms in the 1915 Lanterman House in La Cañada-Flintridge, California (open to the public), the dining room has original creamy white woodwork to complement the pale palette of its hand-painted frieze and ceiling decoration. The mottled texture of the sponge-painted backgrounds softens the edges of the artfully drawn elements. In the frieze, sprays of grapevines float between scrolling borders; the ceiling design has a simpler, more architectural quality.

☙ 38. *(above, right)* From the 1914–1915 catalog of James Davis Artistic Paper Hangings, this frieze has a row of panels at the top that connect to shieldlike extensions. Between the "shields," the plain background areas make interesting shapes of their own; they are each centered on narrow vertical borders that panelize the wainscot. The design mixes leaves with oranges and the more typical grapes.

🐚 39. Set off by finely crafted red mahogany woodwork, an original wallpaper frieze has survived beautifully in this 1911 dining room. Against a rich teal blue background, its continuous fruit-laden garland motif was designed to mimic the effects of hand painting and stenciling in the far less costly medium of wallpaper.

❦ 40. *(left)* The redwood-paneled dining room of the 1907 Evans House in Marin County, California, has survived with both its original frieze and ceiling wallpaper intact. A machine-woven fabric with a stylized landscape pattern (now quite faded) was used for the room's frieze. Shallow box beams frame ceiling panels of a textured wallpaper resembling burlap; its metallic gold finish (now darkened with age) was intended to reflect light. Original sconces remain, but the ceiling fixture is a 1920s replacement of the first one.

❦ 41. In this detail of the textile frieze seen in Figure 40, its shaded, overlaid motifs of rounded trees and rolling hills are quite discernible despite the fading that has compromised the original color scheme. Revealing the deeper shades of green and gold (with black and purple accents) that it once had, a piece of matching fabric that was stored (away from light) in the attic has survived to document the richer effect of its unfaded condition.

🐾 42. Made of a woven tapestry-type fabric, this richly detailed landscape frieze is original to a 1911 dining room's decorative scheme. Most of the leafy "tapestry" patterns that were popular for bungalows were far smaller in scale than this, and most were likely to be of wallpaper made to resemble fabric. The frieze colors, now somewhat faded, remain in harmony with the quarter-sawn oak woodwork. Other original, high-budget items here are the iridescent glass light shades and elegant classical moldings that underscore the box-beamed ceiling.

🐨 43. The simple tile facing of the fireplace shows a restraint absent in the ornate gilded lighting and other rich features of this 1912 dining room. Recently added, the frieze reproduces a 1906 Art Nouveau design and is made of Lincrusta, a deeply embossed, linoleum-like wall covering. Like the lighter-weight embossed paper (Anaglypta) on the ceiling, it is made in England; both have a hand-painted finish. Above the fireplace, a panel reproduces one repeat of a large-scale wallpaper frieze design of 1900 by Walter Crane.

🐨 44. Viewed through a colonnade that divides it from the living room, this dining room shines, but white paint once covered all its original fir wood-work. Refinished with a deep mahogany-colored stain, its good "bungalow bones" are renewed. Scant wall space above the large built-in side-board determined that a narrow wall-paper border above an overall pattern would best fit the room. Inspired by the period ceiling papers with gold ink that reflected light (see Figure 40), this ceiling got a metallic gold-painted finish instead. Vintage wooden chairs surround a library table that became a dining table (which can seat eight) by the clever addition of a glass top.

🐾 45 & 46. Before and after views of a 1913 dining room prove that original woodwork alone does not ensure an appropriate decorating scheme. In the first view, the plain white frieze space and ceiling do not interact at all with the woodwork. At the very least, a more flattering paint color would help, but a period-style pattern, along with some color, would be a more promising solution. Wallpaper has long been argued as a viable alternate to stenciling or hand-painted finishes, and the homeowners here became convinced. In the subsequent view, the wallpaper frieze that they selected (a recent adaptation of an English Arts and Crafts design by W. Dennington) features a procession of colorful, strutting peacocks. A soft, creamy paint color was used to create a gentle transition from the frieze to the ceiling.

🐝 47 & 48. Before and after views of a 1914 dining room show that it suffered from problems similar to those that beset the dining room in Figure 45. Stark white paint on the available wall and ceiling areas did nothing to unite the room's elements. As the later photograph illustrates, a few well-chosen period-style wallpapers can make a big difference. Eradicating any trace of white wall or ceiling areas, the papers pull the room's parts together yet still appear appropriately subordinate to its strong architectural elements. Printed on a warm, neutral paper that flatters the wood tones around it, the new scheme's key component is the frieze. Its large-scale geometric "pendant" design effectively counterbalances the box-beamed ceiling. The ceiling panels feature a period-style treatment with a textured metallic gold background paper intended to reflect light. Narrow borders framing the ceiling panels match the frieze (as do the oak-leaf corner blocks that accent some of the panels).

BUNGALOW BACKGROUND

America's most popular house of the early twentieth century, the bungalow, is making a big comeback as our newest "historic" house. Surviving bungalows are now considered treasures by historic preservationists, while homeowners rediscover the bungalow's appeal as a modest, practical home with a convenient floor plan. This book highlights an important aspect of bungalow interiors.

Webster's New Collegiate Dictionary describes a bungalow as "a dwelling of a type first developed in India, usually one story, with low sweeping lines and a wide verandah." The word *bungalow* derives from the Hindi *bangala,* both an old Hindu kingdom in the Bengal region of India and a rural Bengali hut with a high thatched-roof overhang creating a covered porch (or verandah) around the perimeter to provide shade from the scorching sun. The height and steep pitch of the roof encouraged the hottest air to rise and escape, while cooler air flowed in at ground level (especially after sundown). The British colonists adapted the design in their own dwellings, and their success spread the concept from India to elsewhere in the British Empire, especially Southeast Asia, Africa, New Zealand, and Australia. By the late eighteenth century, the name *bangala* had been anglicized to *bungalow.*

This name first appeared in print in the United States in 1880.

Used in an architectural journal, it described a single-story, shingled Cape Cod summerhouse ringed by covered porches. By the 1900s, *bungalow* had become part of our popular vocabulary, at first associated with vacation homes, both seaside and mountain. The bungalow's informality, a refreshing contrast to stuffy Victorian houses, helped fuel its popularity as a year-round home. It had its greatest fame as a modest middle-class house from 1900 to 1930.

Widely promoted, the bungalow was touted for its modernity, practicality, affordability, convenience, and often-artistic design. Expanding industry and a favorable economy across the country created an urgent need for new, affordable, middle-class housing, which the bungalow was just in time to meet.

In America, a bungalow implied a basic plan, rather than a specific style, of modest house. Typically, it consisted of 1,200 to 1,500 square feet, with living room, dining room, kitchen, two bedrooms, and bathroom all on one level. Some bungalows had roomy attic quarters, but most attics were bare or intended to be developed as the family's needs grew. A bungalow set in a garden fulfilled many Americans' dream of a home of their own.

Widely publicized California bungalows in the early 1900s spawned frenzied construction in booming urban areas across the country. In design, most bungalows built prior to World War I adopted the so-called Craftsman style, sometimes combined with influences from the Orient, the Swiss chalet, or the Prairie style. After the war, public taste shifted toward historic housing styles, and bungalows adapted Colonial Revival, English cottage, Tudor, Mission, and Spanish Colonial Revival features.

Today Craftsman is the style most associated with bungalows. Characterized inside and out by use of simple horizontal lines, Craftsman style relies on the artistry of exposed wood joinery (often visible on front porch detailing). Natural or rustic materials (wood siding, shingles, stone, and clinker brick) are favored. Interiors may be enriched with beamed ceilings, high wainscot paneling, art glass, and hammered copper or metalwork lighting accents.

The word *Craftsman* was coined by prominent furniture manufacturer and tastemaker Gustav Stickley, who used it to label his line of sturdy, slat-backed furniture (also widely known as Mission style), which was influenced by the English Arts and Crafts movement. That movement developed in the mid-nineteenth century as a reaction against the Industrial Revolution. Early leaders such as John Ruskin and William Morris turned to the medieval past for inspiration as they sought to preserve craft skills disappearing in the wake of factory mechanization.

In both the decorative arts (furniture, wallpaper, textiles, glass, metalwork, and ceramics) and architecture, the Arts and Crafts movement advocated use of the finest natural materials to make practical and beautiful designs, executed with skillful handcraftsmanship. One goal was to improve the poor-quality, mass-produced home furnishings available to the rising middle class. Morris and a group of like-minded friends founded a business to produce well-designed, handcrafted goods for domestic interiors. Although the company aspired to make its goods affordable to all, it faced the inevitable conflict between quality and cost. However, its Arts and Crafts example inspired many others in England (and eventually in America) to relearn treasured old craft traditions and continue them for posterity.

As it grew, the movement also became involved in politics, pressing for social reforms. Factory workers trapped in dull, repetitive jobs (with little hope for anything better) were among their chief concerns; they saw the workers' fate as a waste of human potential and talent.

The idealistic and visionary English movement's artistic goals of design reform were more successful than its forays into social reform. Perhaps its greatest success, in both England and the United States, was in giving the public a renewed sense of the value of quality materials, fine craftsmanship, and good design in times of rapid world change.

The Arts and Crafts movement had multiple influences on the American bungalow. The movement arrived here from England in the early 1900s, just as the bungalow was becoming popular. Among its most successful promoters was Elbert Hubbard, founder of the Roycroft Community, a group of artisans producing handmade books and decorative arts inspired by Morris. Hubbard also published two periodicals and sold goods by mail order.

Gustav Stickley was another American inspired by England's important reform movement and soon was expressing this inspiration in the sometimes austere but well-made designs of his Craftsman style. Becoming an influential promoter of the bungalow as an ideal "Craftsman home," he marketed furniture, lighting, metalwork, and textiles styled appropriately for it. His magazine, *The Craftsman,* was a popular vehicle for his ideas and products, and he sold plans for the Craftsman houses he published in his magazine. The wide popularity of his Craftsman style spread the aesthetic sensibilities of the Arts and Crafts movement into countless American middle-class households, making it a growing influence on architecture and decorative arts here. (England in the early twentieth century remarkably had no middle-class housing form comparable to the American bungalow, but Australia has bungalows of that period, inspired by ours, rather than any from Britain.)

Other manufacturers eventually contributed to Stickley's downfall by blatantly copying his ideas and products and eroding his market share. Once Stickley's exclusive brand name, the word *Craftsman* was assimilated into general use and became public property after his bankruptcy in 1916.

Americans choosing the Craftsman style for their homes, interiors, and furnishings rarely were committed to the artistic and philosophical reforms of the Arts and Crafts movement; most were simply following a vogue. Prospective homeowners (and real estate developers) usually selected their bungalow designs from inexpensive sets of plans marketed in catalogs called plan books; few used an architect's services. Some people even bought prefabricated "ready-cut" or "kit" houses. First sold in 1909 by Sears, Roebuck and Company, prefabricated houses soon were widely copied. In the heat of bungalow mania, Sears and others offered tempting incentives to prospective bungalow buyers, such as bonus financing for their lots. For a time, it was said that if you had a job, you could afford a bungalow. But when jobs were in short supply as the Great Depression hit, many defaulted on their little dream homes, leaving their creditors stung.

The depression ended the heyday of the bungalow, but its practical innovations reappeared in later houses, then more likely to be called cottages. The post-World War II ranch house could be considered the legacy of the bungalow. Only recently has a rising demand for lower-cost houses triggered a reevaluation of vintage bungalow stock as viable housing. In response to public demand, the home planning and construction industries have reprised some of the obvious charms of the bungalow in new homes. A real boon for homeowners seeking to restore or renovate a vintage bungalow (or perhaps build a new one) is today's flourishing Arts and Crafts revival, fueled by the demand for a wide array of newly crafted home furnishings that reflect the traditions and spirit of the Arts and Crafts movement.

CREDITS

Figure 5: Pillow by Dianne Ayres, Arts & Crafts Period Textiles. **Figure 11:** Architectural renovation by The Johnson Partnership, Seattle, Washington. **Figure 13:** Restoration architect: Martin Eli Weill; designer/collection curator: Roger L. Conant. **Figure 14:** Fixture by Arroyo Craftsman Lighting. **Figure 24:** Ceiling fixture by Arroyo Craftsman Lighting. **Figures 26–27:** Renovation by Jarvis Architects, Oakland, California. **Figure 28:** Wallpaper by Bradbury & Bradbury; table runners by Dianne Ayres, Arts & Crafts Period Textiles. **Figure 29:** Lighting by Michael Adams/Aurora Studios. **Figure 30:** Curtains by Dianne Ayres, Arts & Crafts Period Textiles. **Figure 31:** Decorative painting by Lynne McDaniel. **Figure 34:** Wallpaper frieze by Victorian Collectibles; installed by Gary Yuschalk and Larkin Mayo; decorative wall painting by Woody Vermeire. **Figure 35:** Chair by Debey Zito Fine Furniture. **Figure 43:** Wallpaper frieze by Bradbury & Bradbury; Lincrusta and Anaglypta by Crown Corporation; installed by Peter Bridgman; decorative painting by Joni Monnich. **Figure 44:** Wallpaper by Bradbury & Bradbury. **Figure 46:** Wallpaper by Bradbury & Bradbury; installed by Helen Boutell. **Figure 48:** Wallpaper by Bradbury & Bradbury; installed by Peter Bridgman.

ARCHIVAL IMAGES

Figures 1–2: Courtesy the collection of Dianne Ayres and Timothy Hansen, Arts & Crafts Period Textiles. **Figures 32–33, 38:** From the collection of Paul Duchscherer.